kids will be kids

kids will be kids

the wisdom of parents and children

edited by sean keogh

Published in the United States in 2006
by Tangent Publications
an imprint of
Axis Publishing Limited
8c Accommodation Road
London NW11 8ED
www.axispublishing.co.uk

Creative Director: Siân Keogh
Editorial Director: Anne Yelland
Production Manager: Jo Ryan
Production Controller: Cécile Lerbiere

ISBN 1-904707-30-0

2 4 6 8 10 9 7 5 3 1

Printed and bound in China

about this book

The wit and wisdom of children are legendary. Children can make us smile without even trying, as they search for words, tell us stories, misunderstand meaning, do their own thing, and generally have a completely different take on life from grown-ups.

This book brings together a selection of amusing and witty anecdotes by children and inspirational words on what being a parent means. The text throughout is accompanied by appropriate, evocative, and gently amusing animal photographs.

This is an ideal gift book for friends, family, and loved ones in need of a daily smile.

about the author

Sean Keogh has worked in publishing for several years, on a variety of books and magazines on a wide range of subjects. From the many hundreds of contributions that were sent to him, including ones from his own children, he has selected the funniest things kids say and what being a parent is all about.

The best way to tell if two people are married is to see if they are shouting at the same children.

Even boys have interesting things to say if you wait long enough.

I love being 10: it's the oldest I've been in my whole life.

Kissing a boy is OK
as long as he's rich.

Sometimes I get so tired
I forget to have a nap.

When mom says no, ask dad.

Kissing makes you
feel squishy inside.

You can't fall in love with someone who has stinky baseball shoes.

Being in love makes you feel warm all over, so it's great for people who don't have heating.

Kissing is the easiest way to steal someone's chewing gum.

Being in love is better
than going to work.

If you're a good kisser your wife might not notice that you haven't emptied the garbage.

Love is when people stare at each other so much their dinner gets cold.

I'll tell you when
I'm asleep, OK?

The best time to get married is when you leave kindergarden.

Lead us not into temptation and deliver us some email.

Love will always
find you…

…I've been hiding from
it since I was five, but the
girls still find me.

Rainbows are just for looking at…

…nobody understands them.

A blizzard is when it snows sideways.

In some rocks you can
find fossil footprints of fishes.

I'm not running around in circles…

…I'm orbiting.

Inertia is when something is moving, then stops, and carries on.

The wind is like air,
only pushier.

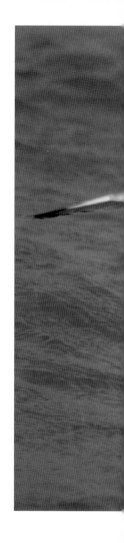

A long time ago lots of dead animals turned into fossils, but some became oil instead.

You can fool some of the people all of the time and all of the people some of the time, but you can never fool your mom.

It's fun being a kid.

It isn't homework unless it's due tomorrow.

When I was a kid my
parents moved a lot, but
I always found them.

Children seldom misquote you. In fact, they usually repeat word for word what you shouldn't have said.

I love to give homemade
gifts. Which one of my
kids would you like?

Kids teach you how
to cope with life.

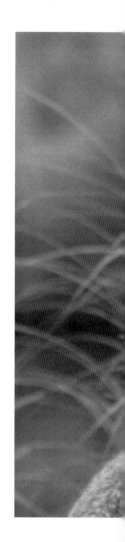

There is only one pretty child in the world…

…and every mother has it.

Children soon forget
your presents, but always
remember your presence.

Who are these kids and
why are they calling
me Dad?

A child's greatest period of growth is the month after you've bought new school clothes.

Anyone who says "Easy as taking candy from a baby" has never tried taking candy from a baby.

Forget money…

…it's better to give your
kids your time.

A child is a reminder that
playtime is an important
part of everyday life.

Nothing you do for your kids is ever wasted.

A child may abandon his ideals,
but an adult never wears
out his short pants.

Feed a child milk and praise
and it will grow tall, strong,
and big-hearted.

Children are linked to adults by the fact that they are turning into them.

The best way to deal with a child is not to be its parent.

Kids don't need

an easy life.

You don't only love your kids because they're your kids—you love them because of the friendship they give you as they grow.

My mother loved children…

…she often said how happy she'd be if she had one.

Don't pit your wits against
a child—you'll lose.

A child's toys are just
what his dad wanted.

Parents were invented
for children to ignore.

Every child is an artist.

You know children are growing up when they start asking questions that have easy answers.

Children don't listen,
but hear everything.

Even a child totally engrossed
in a video will hear you
criticizing Grandma.

It is amazing how quickly the kids learn to drive a car, yet are unable to understand the lawnmower, snow-blower, or vacuum cleaner.

Parents plant magic
in a child's mind.

Love your kids, especially
when they do the opposite
of what you tell them.

To keep your kids, let them go.

If your children look up
to you, you've made a
success of life's biggest job.